RELIGIOUS EDUCATION
IN THE
PRIMARY SCHOOL

ALAN AND ERICA BROWN

The National Society (Church of England)
for Promoting Religious Education

The National Society
Church House
Great Smith Street
London SW1P 3NZ

ISBN 0 901819 47 6

Published 1996 by The National Society (Church of England) for
Promoting Religious Education

© *The National Society (Church of England) for Promoting Religious
Education 1996*

Printed in England by Bourne Press Ltd

Contents

Introduction

This booklet is designed for busy people. It will help RE co-ordinators, headteachers and governors reflect upon the place of RE in the curriculum of their school. It is intended to be a quick but thought-provoking read which will also offer some very practical help in both planning and practice.

The text is aimed at all those concerned with RE in the primary school but some teachers in Church schools may find some parts more relevant than others. It is not possible in such a brief booklet to cover all aspects of RE but the authors hope that the content will build upon the other booklets in this series on RE and complement their previous joint publication *Primary School Worship* (National Society, 1992).

The booklet divides into two sections. The first section considers some questions about RE often asked by primary school teachers and offers general guidance about planning and approaching difficult or controversial aspects of RE. The second part contains, by way of illustrative example, some ideas to help with classroom practice. The examples are taken from a number of different religions although they concentrate mainly on Christianity, but it is intended that the basic principles enshrined in the approach could be applied to any good RE theme.

Section One

1

Religious Education in the Curriculum

he principal aim for the whole school curriculum as set out in the Education Reform Act 1988 (ERA) is to promote the:

> spiritual, moral, cultural, mental and physical development of pupils and of society, and prepare pupils for the opportunities, responsibilities and experiences of adult life.
>
> Clause 1. (2)(a)

Religious Education is a statutory part of the basic curriculum although, unlike the National Curriculum, it is administered at a local rather than a national level. It has equal standing in relation to the core and other foundation subjects although it is not subject to nationally prescribed attainment targets and assessment procedures.

Religious Education is primarily concerned with three areas namely:

1. spiritual development;

2. a knowledge of the belief and practice of religion; and

3. opportunities to explore religious perspectives on human experience.

Model syllabuses for RE

In 1994 the Schools Curriculum and Assessment Authority (SCAA) published two *model syllabuses* for RE. Although these documents are not statutory, they are designed to provide guidance to Agreed Syllabus Conferences and Standing Advisory Conferences on RE – SACRE – (and not to schools). Many new syllabuses reflect the content of the models, including Programmes of Study based on the beliefs and practices of Christianity and the other principal religions in Great Britain.

The principal world religions

Although legislation does not define which principal religions should be taught, it has come to be accepted that all principal religions in Great Britain should be included and children should learn *about and from* the religions studied. Traditionally, there are six major world religions normally studied in Great Britain, namely: Christianity, Islam, Hinduism, Buddhism, Sikhism and Judaism.

Most Agreed Syllabuses for RE are united in the view that, in the early years of pupils' religious and spiritual development, teaching should be relevant to children's life experiences whilst also encouraging an awareness and understanding of the belief and practice of religion.

A differentiated approach to learning

A differentiated approach to learning which treats pupils as individuals should apply in RE. *This will include:*

- the delivery of carefully structured teaching approaches;

- providing imaginative learning experiences which arouse and sustain children's interest;

- supporting the learning which takes place in RE by what is taught in other curriculum areas.

The spiritual dimension of RE

The National Curriculum Council Discussion Paper, *Spiritual and Moral Education: a discussion paper* (NCC, 1993; SCAA, 1996), argues that spiritual development is 'fundamental to other areas of learning'. In the context of *religion* this may include beliefs and a sense of awe or transcendence. But spirituality is also concerned with the very essence of *what it means to be human* and in this sense it includes self-understanding and self-worth, creativity, emotional responses, a personal quest for meaning and purpose and the forming of relationships.

Religious perspectives on human experience

Study units in the early stages of pupils' RE may contain little which is explicitly religious at all, but children's own life experiences provide an essential framework for understanding religion. All children come to school with experiences of relationships with those people who care for them. Within the school family they will need encouragement to respond to their learning in a way which nurtures positive attitudes towards themselves and towards other people.

Knowledge and understanding of religious belief and practice

For children to begin to understand something about the belief which lies at the heart of religious practice they will need to learn *about* religion as well as learn *from* religion. Although many children may come from homes where religion is not a way of life, others will learn about faith and practice in their families through such things as the clothes which they wear, the food which they eat or the objects and symbols which surround them.

Key Stage 1

At Key Stage 1 RE should strive to build on children's understanding of themselves and their experiences of family life and relationships. It is important that teachers take the variety of children's experience into account when planning schemes of work. All pupils should learn that they are personally valued from the attitudes which they encounter in school, while they also begin to discover the contribution which other people make. They should become increasingly aware of things which are special and important to themselves and other people. Children will benefit from opportunities to develop their awareness of the local environment through journeys and visits and by having a chance to experience awe and wonderment in the natural world. They should be introduced to symbolism in religion and hear stories about the lives of key figures and religious leaders.

Pupils should be encouraged to celebrate their own achievements and milestones as well as sharing a variety of occasions when people meet together for worship and festivals. Some children will find it very difficult to enter imaginatively into the experience of other people and they may need help in order to be aware of the needs and desires of their peers and their teachers.

Key Stage 2

Key Stage 2 should enhance the opportunities and experiences which pupils have already encountered in order that they may build on their knowledge and understanding of religion and increase their spiritual and moral development. Children should be developing a greater understanding of themselves and an awareness of the needs and feelings of other people from a variety of faiths and cultures. They should be given an opportunity to interact with the natural world and the local environment. By the end of Key Stage 2 pupils should have been helped to explore a range of religious ideas and themes including how these are communicated through sacred writings and symbols. They should have heard stories about the life and teaching of Jesus and other religious figures and have been given opportunities to consider their own questions and concerns arising from the Programmes of Study. Their knowledge of religious belief and practice will grow through activities such as visiting places of worship and meeting people from religious communities.

The scheme of work for RE

In order that the RE taught in school reflects a curriculum which is broad and balanced, the content will need to be planned carefully whilst also being relevant to the life experiences and individual learning needs of pupils. A scheme of work is an essential tool in the planning process but if it is to meet the specific needs of individual children it will have to be interpreted and implemented creatively through the opportunities for learning which are provided.

The schemes of work illustrated later in this booklet draw on the content of the SCAA Model Syllabuses and use the two Attainment Targets: 'A knowledge and understanding of religious belief and practice, and 'Religious perspectives on human experience'. Teachers should choose content from both and provide learning experiences which are appropriate to children's ability. Background information is provided for each Programme of Study but some non-specialist colleagues may benefit from the further reading suggested at the end of this booklet.

2

Questions Teachers Raise

WHY TEACH RE AT ALL?

Why indeed? Parents can withdraw their children from it, teachers can withdraw from teaching it (except in voluntary aided schools) so why bother? Yet oddly, it is the one school subject that captures the headlines in the press time and time again. Perhaps it catches in the conscience of the nation which, while not wishing to practise religion to any serious intentional degree, wants to ensure that its children are injected with sufficient understanding of religion to know what it is about.

There continues to be a general misunderstanding of RE that it is inculcation *into* religion (or *a* religion) rather than a study of religion in itself. In one sense *all* teaching is concerned with indoctrination because teachers socialise children, teach them by example and, crudely, schools cannot run unless there is a moral framework acknowledged by all and accepted by the vast majority. So many schools, whether they are Church schools or not, make assumptions about the nature of the RE they intend to teach. For many teachers the home background of their pupils will be of central significance and they would not only expect their young pupils to bring their home to school but they would not wish to do anything which would contravene the religions and spiritual values of the pupil's family.

The *real* reason to teach RE is that most people in the world are religious. They may not be very devout, some may move in and out of their religion from time to time or even change their religion. Some religious people will be tolerant of others, some will not and there will be enormous diversity and debate within every religion.

Pupils cannot be unaware of the claims religion makes on people throughout the world. There is so much on the television and in the

8

media generally that religion leaps out at them. It is very likely that, depending upon where they live, on their way to school they will pass churches, chapels, mosques, gurdwaras etc.

WILL TEACHING RE HELP PUPILS DEVELOP TOLERANCE AND RESPECT?

It would be wonderful if it were so simple. The principal aim of RE should be to help pupils understand religion and one might hope that tolerance and respect would grow from that. One has to take care that we do not make claims that are too grandiose. Surely *all* education should help pupils grow in respect for the integrity of other people, their beliefs and ways of life. Knowledge of different religions, or even different denominations, does not automatically create respect, but meeting people of integrity, listening to sincerely held beliefs different from one's own, being open enough to listen, to discuss and to learn can help develop respect.

The history of religion has not always been graced with peace and respect, so one could hope that helping pupils to recognise the integrity of spirituality within people of different faiths would be a major contribution to a deeper sense of understanding and greater sensibility to people's religious convictions. Pupils deserve to receive accurate information about people's various beliefs so whatever judgements they arrive at they are at least based on correct information.

HOW CAN I TEACH SOMETHING I DON'T BELIEVE IN?

The temptation is to say, 'Easily – but with discernment', but it is not quite so easy as that. Religions do have their own structures and while they may share some spiritual insights, they can be very protective of their distinctive beliefs and values. One should be aware, however, that prejudice and division are alive and well and living within each religion. Some Protestants would find it very difficult to teach Roman Catholic beliefs and practices because they

9

believe them to be wrong – and this is, one hopes, an age of ecumenism.

Some Christians find it difficult to teach about other faiths, not because they don't believe in them, but because they feel their teaching may be inadequate and may not do justice to them.

SCAA produced two Model Syllabuses in 1994 in which they provided two useful phrases which might help such teachers: 'Learning about' and 'Learning from' (see above p. 5).

Briefly, 'learning about' helps teachers of all persuasions to realise that we all learn about 'things' and some of those 'things' we do not agree with i.e. slavery, apartheid, genocide etc. We teach about them in history or geography or ethics and are able to suspend our feelings about them while we help young pupils reflect upon the consequences of such beliefs and actions. So how much *easier* it is to teach about things in which one does not believe, but which do bring positive values and affirm life for thousands of millions of people.

'Learning from' also helps teachers to recognise that knowledge (and belief) is only a part of a pupil's education. All of us are touched in some way by what, and how, we learn, and for pupils to be open to the educational process they will need to be grazed and touched in some way by the things they learn.

We do not live in an isolated village. The media opens us to violence, conflict, tragedy, disaster and excitement from all over the world. It also brings us the rich colour of diversity and the energetic enthusiasm of the committed faithful from across the world. To learn 'from' is to touch the next century.

HOW CAN I TEACH RE WHEN I DON'T KNOW EVERYTHING ABOUT RELIGION?

Well, yes, that is a pretty persuasive argument and one feels concern for teachers who, in addition to teaching the whole of the National Curriculum, also have to teach RE. How can they indeed be experts in every field? Many primary school teachers will have had a very small part of their initial training on RE. Most will rely

10

on the schools RE co-ordinator (have *you* got one?) to help them. Some local authorities offer good close support for teachers as do many dioceses, but some do not and it is unreasonable to expect high quality teaching from all staff when no support is forthcoming from the local authorities.

Still, what can one do? In moments of crisis remember the following ten points:

- *Don't* teach anything you haven't researched and resourced.

- *Don't* remember the stories you were told when you were at school and simply repeat them. Life has moved on.

- *Don't* force RE into a topic that doesn't offer it a chance.

- *Don't* think in stereotypes. Religious people of whatever religion are all different and this diversity can be a great joy (and a life-saver).

- *Don't* allow your negative opinions – or your prejudices – to stand in the way of the pupils. There is a vast area of religious and spiritual insight available to pupils and you are the means of entry. Tread with care.

- *Do* read a simple but interesting book on the subject. Some of the GCSE textbooks will provide primary teachers with sufficient information to spark off their innate creativity. (This is heresy to the RE purists but it works.)

- *Do* have clear objectives. *What* do you want the pupils to do, to learn, to reflect on etc.

- *Do* read the story (if you're telling one) first and look up the background to it. Then decide on your objectives (see above).

- *Do* ask for help – a colleague, someone from a nearby religious community, a parent. Surprisingly, a lot of people are religious and most are willing to offer support.

- *Do* take heart and recognise you might get some things wrong but they can be put right together with the pupils. Pupils and teacher can find out in partnership and share success and failure.

3

Planning Schemes of Work

HOW DO I CHOOSE A SCHEME OF WORK?

F or most teachers the Agreed Syllabus or Diocesan Guidelines will provide some good examples, and further schemes of work can also be found in Section Two of this booklet. Basically, one can decide whether a scheme has any true mileage in it for RE by applying the following criteria:

- are there different levels of understanding and distinctive skills and concepts to be developed?

- is the scheme central to the beliefs and/or practices of a religion?

- is there an opportunity for pupils to learn *about* a religion and *from* a religion?

Otherwise, the same educational strategies apply:

- one should try to reduce the emphasis on simply transmitting information, although that does have a significant place.

- recognise that while whole-class teaching can have its merits, to teach in small groups helps share resources and can assist with differentiation.

- plan a variety of tasks, not just writing out a story or drawing a picture. There are some excellent books and resources available to help: planning visits, using religious artifacts; using posters, large and small.

- allow time for and plan for pupils to discuss the topic or scheme of work. You can still have clear objectives for such 'open-ended' discussions. Pupils are reflective, creative, and not inert or static; they evolve all the time, so pupils need to explore fundamental questions and not just learn what the traditional religious questions (and answers) have been.

WHAT SHOULD AN RE CO-ORDINATOR DO?

Another ten items to make up a check list.

- Establish how much money will be available in the school development plan for RE; how much time will be available (aim at 5 per cent); what in-service provision will be needed for you and the rest of the staff.

- Know what the legal requirement is for RE; what SCAA recommends and have your *own* copy of the Agreed Syllabus/Diocesan Guidelines *in addition* to the school's copy.

- Carry out an RE audit i.e. assess, with colleagues, their strengths and weaknesses with regard to teaching RE; review the resources available to staff and pupils (including the library); examine the recent work done by the pupils with regard to progression, differentiation and assessment.

- Ensure that RE in the school has clear, well stated and agreed aims; draw up objectives for each scheme of work. Ensure the assessment objectives are stated and the learning outcomes are clear.

- Become familiar with resources in the area around the school – RE centres, libraries, places of worship, specific individuals and communities. Don't forget to liaise with other primary schools and nearby secondary schools whom you feed.

- Persuade the school to subscribe to an RE journal like *RE Today* or *Respect* in order to help spread good practice and build up a library of ideas.

- Provide support for some good displays of work in RE. There are also many attractive posters now available and a display of interesting, colourful pupil books will have an immediate interest for pupils, teachers and visitors.

- Gather together a collection of resources on schemes of work taught in the school. Boxes of resources on holy books, places of worship, festivals etc. make RE much more accessible for teachers and pupils.

- Trace a 'pupil path' through the Key Stages 1 and 2. Make a list of what they will actually do and a second list of what types of learning experiences they will have. Do these lists appear to provide pupils with a rounded view of religion? Is there anything missing? Is there a reasonably healthy balance between 'learning about' and 'learning from'?

- Particularly at Key Stage 1, has the school offered the pupils opportunities to:

  - enjoy stories and festivals;

  - develop a sense of awe and wonder at the natural and technological world;

  - develop a sense of community and belonging?

Michael Kincaid in his book *Learning in RE* (Hodder & Stoughton, 1991, p. ix) offers the following seven points which are of immeasurable help to the teacher:

(i) If learning is to be effective for all students, we need to implement a view of learning which sees students as possessing a set of abilities open to continuous improvement, rather than having a general ability which is fixed and unalterable.

(ii) Since students come to new learning with different stocks of these abilities, their success or failure and subsequent motivation depends on the use of a variety of teaching styles as well as differentiated treatment.

(iii) If learning RE is to be effective for all students it must be developed in a structured way. That structure should be recognisable and intelligible to students and not only to teachers.

(iv) If learning RE is to be relevant, it must be seen to be contributing to students' personal development over a

14

number of elements, but particularly to their search for meaning and value.

(v) An important element in students' personal development is the ability to take decisions in the moral sphere. Religious education has a major role in delivering moral education in the curriculum.

(vi) Personal development is essentially a process. Crucial to that process is the growing ability to evaluate. Specific measures need to be taken to help students learn and evaluate.

(vii) Effective learning requires the setting of achievable targets linked to appropriate methods and resources. These should be brought together in a way that allows students to experience success at regular intervals.

4

Learning About and
Learning From Christianity

I believe that Christianity is by and large . . . the worst
taught of the great religions . . . much of the traditional
teaching of Christianity has proceeded on false
assumptions and has been quite unrealistic. It has been
biblically based without any real attempt to see how
the Bible has functioned in various Churches and in
human experience. It has cut out great swathes of the
tradition because of ideological attitudes. It has done
very little to illuminate the range of Christian experience.

Professor Ninian Smart in *Teaching Christianity*
(ed. Clive Ericker, Lutterworth, 1994, p. viii)

One of the problems that arises when teaching Christianity is that
many teachers simply teach from their memory of what they were
taught when they were at school. Some also believe that while they
know little about the other faiths, they know quite enough about
Christianity.

The Board of Education of the Church of England produced the
following guidelines for teaching Christianity. The intention was to
provide clear end of Key Stage statements on what should be taught
to pupils and what learning opportunities pupils might expect to
experience.

THE BIBLE

Key Stage 1

Pupils should be able to:

- identify some stories from the Bible;

- recognise Christmas and Easter stories;

- demonstrate awareness that the Bible is a special book for Christians;

- know why Christians read and listen to the Bible;

- respond imaginatively to stories from the Bible.

Key Stage 2

Pupils should be able to:

- demonstrate some awareness of how the Bible grew;

- look up references in the Bible;

- demonstrate knowledge and understanding of some key material from the Old and New Testaments;

- demonstrate a knowledge of some of the ways Christians use the Bible in life and worship;

- reflect on and respond imaginatively to Biblical material.

JESUS

Key Stage 1

Pupils should be able to:

- demonstrate knowledge of key events in the life of Jesus;

- give an example of a story Jesus told;

- demonstrate awareness of the effect Jesus had on the people who met him;

- explain how Christians remember Jesus in worship;

- recognise the cross and crucifix as Christian symbols;

- be able to offer an opinion about an aspect of Jesus's teaching.

Key Stage 2

Pupils should be able to:

- demonstrate familiarity with the life of Jesus as outlined in St Mark's or St Luke's Gospels;

- explain the connection between key events in the life of Jesus and major Christian festivals;

- demonstrate some understanding of key ideas about Jesus held by Christians;

- demonstrate an ability to reflect on the teaching of Jesus;

- demonstrate some understanding of the importance of Jesus for Christians;

- recognise and name important Christian symbols and give a simple explanation of their meaning;

- explain some of the ways in which Christians remember Jesus in worship.

THE CHURCH

Key Stage 1

Pupils should be able to:

- name correctly some essential features of a church building and explain their use;

- identify why a church is a special place for Christians;

- begin to understand that the Church is a collection of people and not just a building;

18

- identify connections between the building and the activities which take place there;

- respond imaginatively to the building.

Key Stage 2

Pupils should be able to:

- recognise some differences and similarities between two different places of Christian worship;

- show understanding of the relationship between the worship and the form of the building;

- demonstrate understanding of how Christians in the Church see themselves as members of a community;

- reflect on the need for believers to have a special place of worship;

- show understanding of how members of the Christian community feel about their building, and why.

CHRISTIAN FESTIVALS

Key Stage 1

Pupils should be able to:

- demonstrate familiarity with stories relating to Christmas and Easter;

- respond imaginatively to stories of Christmas and Easter;

- demonstrate an awareness of how Christians celebrate Christmas and Easter;

- identify key features of at least two other Christian special times, e.g. Advent, Mothering Sunday, Pentecost, Ascension.

Key Stage 2

Pupils should be able to:

- identify the major festivals and other special times of the Christian year; their relation to each other; their celebration and significance for Christians;

- know and comment on the symbols connected with those festivals;

- demonstrate an awareness of the different ways in which different groups of Christians may celebrate the same festival.

CHRISTIAN WORSHIP

Key Stage 1

Pupils should be able to:

- demonstrate knowledge of some significant features of worship;

- recognise and identify some well-known Christian prayers and hymns;

- make some connection between belief in God and worship;

- recognise that Jesus is the focal point of Christian worship.

Key Stage 2

Pupils should be able to:

- demonstrate understanding of the basic form and importance of the Eucharist;

- demonstrate awareness of forms of worship used to mark rites of passage;

- demonstrate understanding and some knowledge of ritual;

- demonstrate an understanding of the use of symbols in worship;

- identify and recognise responses of joy, sadness, thanksgiving, penitence and reconciliation;

- recognise some well-known prayers, including the Lord's Prayer.

BELIEF, FAITH AND VALUES

Key Stage 1

Pupils should be able to:

- comment on the events and characters in some of the parables;

- demonstrate a knowledge of the lives of some famous Christians;

- demonstrate an awareness of the importance of forgiveness;

- identify the moral in a simple Biblical and/or Christian story.

Key Stage 2

Pupils should be able to:

- identify the importance of morality in the teaching of the Bible;

- comment on the importance of Jesus in the lives of Christian believers;

- demonstrate knowledge of how and why Christians communicate their faith;

- demonstrate the diversity of views among Christians on some moral issues;

- give examples of the ways in which people show that their faith is important to them;

21

- give examples of ways in which Christian belief has made a profound difference to the lives of individuals.

These are bare bones or, if you prefer, a scaffolding upon which to build and support RE and the teaching of Christianity. If pupils leave a primary school with this sort of understanding of Christianity then they will have been involved in a lively and informative teaching programme.

5

Some Familiar Problems
when Teaching about Christianity

HOW DO I TEACH ABOUT JESUS?

Different people have advocated so many approaches to the teaching of Christianity in school that it is difficult to know where to begin or where to end. For many years after the 1944 Education Act, RE (or RI, Religious Instruction, as it was then) in schools was essentially Bible stories and/or the study of the Bible texts. Some changes took place in the 1960s when it was believed that the Bible and Christian teaching would only have meaning in young people's lives if they were seen to be relevant. So began an 'issue' style of RE which was designed to amplify, explain, and provide answers for social and moral problems. During the 1970s there began a wave of teaching about world religions, and in the 1980s the Chichester Project pioneered an approach to teaching Christianity in secondary schools based upon the assumption that pupils had no prior knowledge of Christianity at all. Currently there appears to be a vogue for 'spirituality' though this could be an excuse for those who don't wish to use the word 'religion' and enjoy the vague and loose use of the term. That will be examined later.

So far we have considered some of the important aspects of Christianity that might form the basics of a teaching programme. What follows is not directly to do with content – some of that was suggested earlier – but has to do with different approaches to the teaching of Christianity. How many teachers go about it? What sort of emphasis should it have? This list is by no means exhaustive and other people will have other suggestions to make.

Jesus

(a) The person of Jesus is obviously of central importance to Christians; for them Jesus was fully God and fully man. This is a difficult concept for theologians to grasp, never mind young children, but they can provide a different, clearer insight. In a school's approach to teaching about Jesus it is important to recognise that a strong vein in the teaching of the Church has emphasised that it was only because Jesus was human that he could know what it was like to share in life's suffering and problems; Jesus's humanity is as important as his divinity. He is often presented in books, films and stories as a rather distant figure in the sense that everything is too perfect; he floats around, apparently effortlessly, without anxiety, fear or concern. In other words, he is presented in many classrooms as an unreal figure, one who does not share our humanity. This could be controversial, for some Christians believe that emphasis on the humanity of Jesus reduces his divinity and they prefer to represent him as looking different from his contemporaries (see almost any illustration in a book of children's Bible stories). If pupils can become aware of the 'normality' of Jesus – his very human-ness – it becomes easier to understand why Christians believe that God shares in human suffering and human life.

(b) Christians also believe that Jesus came to save humanity from their sins and make salvation possible. Sin, and original sin, is another difficult concept to deal with because it is exem-plified as some form of moral transgression. Is it a sin to speed on the motorway? Some would say it is. Others may say that sin could be whatever prevents a true and honest relationship – it is something which causes estrangement and separation from God. Christians believe that in the story of Adam and Eve in the Garden of Eden there is demonstrated the lack of trust and selfish defiance that caused sin. Most Christians do not believe in the literal truth of that story but interpret it as saying that because of disobedience humans lost their favoured place in the eyes of God. They fell from grace. Only by God's sending of his Son, Jesus, they believe, can human beings regain their place in Paradise. The sin of humanity is removed by the death and resurrection of Jesus. So humans need the grace of God, given through his Son Jesus, in order to restore that sense of true and open relationship. In this way sin can be seen as separation from God and the lack of openness and fullness that is a wholesome part of a true and proper relationship.

The above is a very simple and subjective notion of sin. Most pupils, however, are aware of estrangement and separation; most of them will be aware of doing something which leaves them feeling guilty or upset so that the honesty in a relationship has been lost. They will also be aware that, if the relationship is to be healed, something or someone has to bring the two people together and heal the division. So, in summary, one could approach teaching about Jesus both through his humanity and through the Christian view of sin and the belief that only Jesus's death and resurrection could remove it.

HOW DO I TEACH THE PARABLES AND MIRACLES? DIDN'T THEY HAPPEN A LONG TIME AGO?

Some years ago a student was doing research on fairy tales. She noted they had changed in the (relatively) few years since they had been written by the Brothers Grimm and Hans Christian Andersen, reflecting the changes in society itself. Familiar themes were still present; fear and relief; terror and salvation; good and evil; darkness and light; rich and poor but they were packaged in such a way that they might not easily have been recognised by the original authors.

To raise the question of teaching about parables and miracles through a story about fairy tales is controversial for, to many Christians the parables and miracles of Jesus as they are recorded in the Gospels have far greater meaning than any fairy tale. Yet there are some similarities and it can be a relief to the class teacher if some of these are borne in mind.

–   We do not know the original context of the parable or miracle, we only know where it is recorded in the Gospels. So the original meaning of the parable or the force of the miracle is not always clear.

–   Parables are not very common in the Old Testament but at the time of Jesus they were a very common way of teaching by the Jewish scholars. So the form of teaching used and the various points they raised would be open to debate and discussion. They were points of stimulus in order to acquire greater understanding.

–   Whilst the fairy tale is made up for pleasure, the parables of Jesus have a deeply religious focus although they are not set in concrete. There is some licence given through the telling of the story to engage the art of the story teller, for these stories have been translated many times:

●   Jesus told the parable in (probably) Aramaic.

●   Somebody heard and remembered it.

●   The parable was eventually written down in either Aramaic or Greek or perhaps Hebrew. The parable emerged in a Gospel – written in Greek.

●   The Greek was eventually translated into twentieth-century English.

How should we teach parables?

Parables are to be heard and explored. Some of them are good stories, others are really no more than 'one liners'. Children need to hear them and to explore them within their own experience of life. The stories remain constant but as children grow into young adults their experiences change.

We should remember that some of the parables are set in a pastoral environment some 2,000 years ago in a far off land. They will need explaining. Some like the Prodigal (or Lost) Son have strong overtones of peer-group jealousy which all children experience. Similarly perhaps the 'Good Samaritan' is really about those who choose to ignore the suffering of others (or about the innkeeper who tended the injured man).

How should we teach miracles?

The word normally used in the Gospels for 'miracle' has the meaning 'power' – (we get the word 'dynamite' from it). In St John's Gospel the word most often used means 'sign'. So one could argue that the miracles attributed to Jesus are signs of power on which the observers have to reflect. Also, in Jesus's day people were used to healers so the actions of Jesus were typical of his time. His healing of the blind, deaf and lame could be regarded as a symbol (or a sign) that with understanding a person is made whole.

Miracles point to a world we cannot fully understand. But they can also help pupils to discover that the world is full of awe and wonderment and that even the most eminent of scientists do not hold all the answers. There is much to explore and to explain and miracles are a 'staging post', a point on the infinite line of understanding more about the world and the universe. If as teachers we close the miracles down and do not allow time for reflection and exploration and the creative minds of youngsters to respond, we sell our pupils short.

What do we say?

'Honesty is the best policy' is not always the case in life! But in responding to pupils' questions it usually is. We need to answer questions such as 'Do you believe it?' or 'Did it really happen?'. But in common with most education it is not the actual answer which is important. Rather it is the way in which teachers' answers move the pupil on. Responses which stop at 'Yes' or 'No' do nothing to open up the issues at the heart of the parable or the miracle. 'No I don't believe it myself, but I do see how some Christians think it is important' is the beginning of an exploration.

For Christians all parables and miracles are rooted in history i.e. they all emerge from a particular time. Yet for most Christians they also point beyond an historical moment to an eternal truth which should be discussed with children of all ages and abilities.

Jesus is not the prince who fights through the thorny thickets to awaken the princess with a kiss, nor is the world a place where everything is 'happy ever after'. But the parables and miracles are the result of the keen observer's eye, and they comment on the good as well as the harsher realities of life. Perhaps most of all they acknowledge the struggles which most of us encounter from time to time.

WHAT SHOULD I TEACH ABOUT THE GOSPELS?

(a)   A third of St Mark's Gospel and substantial parts of the others are taken up with the account of Jesus's death. It does Christianity no service to ignore this section of the narrative in order to concentrate on the 'gentle Jesus, meek and mild' approach still so common in some classrooms (see above). To teach only parables and miracles is to ignore what is, for Christians, the central and unique feature of Jesus – his death and resurrection.

Some teachers object that the narrative is too bloodthirsty, too awful for young pupils. That is one view, but if we hold that we have to recognise that we are not teaching Christianity. We are propounding a sort of Christian senti- mentality which provides no basis for further teaching. Pupils will take from the narrative what is appropriate to their expe- rience, and we should not imagine that because adults see things in one way so will pupils. Sentimentality, and the misapplication of it when teaching from the Bible, is one of the major problems when teaching Christianity in schools. Teachers, including believing Christians, will teach the 'nice' bits but not get to grips with suffering pain and death. This is odd, because much of life – including that of our pupils – is touched with pain and suffering.

28

Such an approach leaves pupils with nothing to grow into. If Christianity is taught as the sentimental Christmas story (which is in marked contrast to either of the actual stories in the Gospels of St Matthew and St Luke) it is no wonder that adolescents find little in the faith that matches their experience; and it appears to have no substance as they grow into young adults.

(b)   The regular performance of the primary school Nativity play gives the impression to pupils that Christmas is the most important Christian festival. Many teachers, including those in Church schools, 'do' Christmas year after year but have never re-read the narratives themselves nor read a decent commentary on them. They are unaware that the narratives are significantly different, have little understanding of why that may be the case and, in truth, simply endorse the notion that the Christmas story is a pre-Christmas pantomime. In fact, of course, Easter is *the* Christian festival of the year but how often is it given the same amount of energy and investment?

If teachers are to teach Christianity properly they will have to adapt a more academic approach to the Biblical text. Could pupils suggest reasons for the different stories? Why cannot a school produce 'the alternative Nativity play' based on one of the narratives? Why do pupils think that St Mark and St John omit any Birth narrative? What would it really be like to be born in a stable? What would it be like to flee from a killer over the mountains? There is an urgent need for a more academic, reflective and creative approach to the central Scripture of Christianity.

(c)   The Gospels record many miracles and parables with the onus normally being put upon the hearers or watchers to respond as they will. Pupils should be encouraged to respond to the stories on the basis of their experience and allowed the integrity of understanding for themselves. Adults must have heard the same story a hundred times, yet they will often find something new in it because of their own experience at the time when the story is told. So some of us will see something new in an old story from time to time. How creative it is for pupils not to be told what a story means but to be allowed to explore the parable or the miracle for something that has meaning or interest for them.

HOW CAN I CONVEY THE FEELING AND EMOTION OF THE CHRISTIAN RELIGION?

(a)   Most of us have been on the history tour of the local church – 'This was built in 1836 – the windows were put in in 1924 . . .'. Yet the Christian religion is not about history (though that has a role, of course); it is about faith and feelings. Many people will not have been in a church so what do they feel like in one? Does it smell? Is there a sense of space? Is it light or dark? Does it feel quiet? What is it like in the pulpit? There are all sorts of questions about the affective (or 'feeling') part of life that pupils should be exploring. Maybe the church 'feels' different at festival times from other times; maybe it is plain, with a Bible open on a table. Why is there a table? Why is the Bible open? All sorts of questions emerge which can lead themselves to creative writing or painting. Simply to touch some of the woodwork or stonework, or to allow the colours from the stained glass windows to fall across the face of a pupil creates something of the 'feel' of a place. And then there is silence.

(b)   There are many Christian prayers and hymns which capture all sorts of feelings: happiness, sadness, glory and pain. There is no indoctrination in looking at prayers and talking about what the person praying was feeling; prayers are often like poems exploring deeper feelings with which pupils will identify and have some sympathy, and they may be able to write their own private prayers or poems which do not necessarily have to be read aloud.

(c)   If Christianity has done nothing else, it has been the vehicle and stimulus of much music and art. So often in our schools we ignore these aspects in RE, yet they are often the medium

30

of Christian spirituality and an expression of the glory of God. Posters or pictures with scenes from the Gospels can be measured against the narratives to see how the painter has interpreted the story. These are many cassettes available of Christian music, traditional and modern, which try to capture this aspect of Christian life and worship.

Diversity

For most pupils it is virtually impossible to understand the differences between the various Christian denominations. Many differences are so theologically entrenched that even adults only have a hazy idea of the reasons for them. It is, however, interesting to look at the ways in which various Christian groups do things. Their initiation rites may take place at different ages; their marriage services will differ; their services will vary; their ministers and priests will wear different clothes. All this is easily accessible and interesting. It also helps pupils to recognise that 'Christian' does not mean 'British', and that Jesus did not speak English. The very diversity helps them to understand that Christianity is a world-wide faith with very individual forms of prayer, worship and emphasis. To help pupils understand what it feels like to be a member of a denomination is an important part of teaching how Churches cope with diversity.

This is not necessarily a complete recipe for teaching Christianity but it does suggest that:

(a)   proper preparation should be made before telling Bible stories;

(b)   teaching about Jesus should not be characterised by sentimentality, and the pain and suffering of his death should not be ignored;

(c)   pupils should be encouraged to look carefully and critically at the Biblical narratives from an early age;

(d)   feelings and emotions are an important aspect of Christian life and worship;

(e)   the arts play a fundamental role in Christian worship;

(f)   Christian diversity is not wrong but can be enriching;

and finally,

(g)   pupils should be allowed to understand at their own level, just as adults understand at theirs.

ISN'T IT CONFUSING TO TEACH A RANGE OF WORLD RELIGIONS?

There is so much misleading information on this subject that, as with the teaching of Christianity, it is difficult to know where to begin and end. An earlier section of the booklet dealt with some of the reasons why carefully thought out and properly planned study of religions other than Christianity will be of benefit to pupils.

There has been criticism of a thematic approach to RE as being 'uneducational' and/or confusing. It must be admitted that some teaching – of any subject – can be confusing but if topics are carefully planned and are appropriate to the age and ability of the pupils the chances of any confusion will be reduced.

To develop the point made earlier, if so many people are religious it is important that religion is studied in school. Religions are different from each other in that their adherents express themselves in different ways, so one of the important aspects of teaching of world religion must be a recognition of that diversity. 'Diversity' here is not a negative term – it only implies differences, and if pupils are to develop notions of tolerance and understanding an important platform upon which those notions should be based will be respect for difference.

One reason why the study of religion is so rich is the very variety of religious belief and practice. In turn this variety is so integral to the different cultures of society that they are impossible to disentangle. Just as British society owes much to its Judaic–Christian heritage, the cultures of India owe much to Hinduism, Islam and Buddhism –and, indeed, to Christianity. How, also, may one begin to learn the history, geography and economic and social structure of the Middle East without studying the religion of Islam?

The church, synagogue, mosque, temple or gurdwara, together with the religious home, are all places of religious nurture. Schools, including Church schools, should recognise that part of the process of education is the exploration of religious diversity. Different beliefs and practices are not challenges to be denied but positive statements of each person's feeling and commitment.

If one is a Christian one cannot ever know what it is really like to be a Sikh, Muslim or Buddhist, but one can respect the nature and depth of the commitment. People should be able to recognise the integrity of the beliefs held by others even if they do not share them. The leap of identification can never really be made, though a hand may be held out, the hand of shared religious conviction, in the recognition that each person's religion, with its beliefs and practice, is important.

When teaching about world faiths, therefore, people should not make crude negative comparisons. They should inform, while recognising the differences that exist. These areas of difference, often controversial and divisive, can make interesting areas of study, for the very nature of the difference encourages pupils to question. Someone once commented that the *really* interesting aspects of RE are in the 'Disagreed Syllabus' not the 'Agreed Syllabus'!

Christianity is a religion, simple yet complex; so, in effect, are all religions. In every case the faith of the believer is paramount and the teaching of world religions in the classroom can make a significant contribution to the recognition of the worth of every human being and the breaking down of the barriers of racism, nationalism and xenophobia.

Section Two

T he following schemes of work, taken from three world religions, are offered as both examples and models of how to plan and approach the teaching of a topic. In such a short booklet they do not cover every aspect of the chosen topic but they suggest resources and approaches that will be helpful. Teachers may keep a record of what has been taught by highlighting the relevant content from the model schemes of work. The list of Further Reading and Resources at the end of this booklet groups items according to their faiths which should also prove helpful.

CELEBRATION

The whole pattern of a school's organisation, curriculum and educational philosophy should be reflected in the way in which it celebrates.

Celebration is an integral part of the culture of civilizations all over the world. Through celebration people express joy and thanksgiving. They link the past with the present and demonstrate hope for the future.

Even very young children will remember celebrations, long after the events of everyday life have been forgotten, because celebration brings a sense of occasion and a break from routine, heightening emotional responses to life.

Life is enriched by celebration, both at home, at school, and in the wider community. Children soon begin to recognise the pattern of events throughout a year and they eagerly anticipate them as times of happiness and togetherness, times for sharing, dancing, playing, eating and dressing up.

Children have a natural capacity for entering into the spirit of celebration. They are quick to realise that celebration brings people together and that it is impossible to celebrate alone.

But in the early years celebration needs to be more than just an excuse to dress up and to eat special food. It misses the mark if there is no hint of the central emotion which singles out the celebration from 'ordinary' days in the school year. It is more a matter of capturing the mystique of purpose and plan that lies behind the celebration and of being in touch with previous generations of celebrants.

The following outlines for celebration draw on Christian, Jewish and Hindu festivals and celebrations. However the broad objectives remain the same across faiths:

Objectives

Through experience of celebration it is hoped that pupils will:

- develop an awareness of the events within communities which are significant to believers;

- develop an awareness of the diversity of human response;

- encourage children to reflect on their own experiences of celebration at home, at school and in the worshipping and wider community;

- acquire an ability to share with others, nurturing attitudes of tolerance and respect.

ADVENT AND CHRISTMAS

Advent marks the beginning of the Christian year. The word Advent comes from a Latin word meaning 'coming' or 'arrival'. Advent prepares for the coming of the Messiah.

The season of Advent begins on the fourth Sunday before Christmas, called 'Advent Sunday'. In the Western church this is always the Sunday nearest the feast of St Andrew, which falls on 30th November. There are four Sundays in Advent before Christmas Day.

Originally Advent was celebrated as a penitential period like Lent but today most of this austerity has gone. However, weddings are still discouraged during Advent and people wishing to get married at this time of year frequently do so on St Catherine's Day (25th

November). The Sunday before Advent (Trinity 25) is traditionally known as 'Stir up Sunday' and although this is often interpreted today as a time to make Christmas cakes and puddings, in fact it refers to the Collect (or prayer) for the day, which begins: 'Stir up, we beseech thee, O Lord, the wills of thy faithful people.'

St Nicholas' Day is on 6th December, and this is the day when many children in mainland Europe receive presents. Also celebrated in mainland Europe is the feast day of St Lucy or Lucia on 13th December. In Sweden the daughter of the family will wear white on St Lucia's Day and, wearing a crown of evergreens and lighted candles on her head, she serves special Lucia cakes to her family.

Christmas Eve falls on 24th December and this day marks the final preparations for the celebration of Jesus's birth on Christmas Day, 25th December.

There are several important days after Christmas Day: 26th December is the feast of St Stephen, the first Christian to die for his faith (see Acts 7. 57–60). 27th December is the feast of the apostle St John and 28th December is the feast of the Holy Innocents (see Matthew 2. 16–17). 1st January is the feast of the Circumcision of Jesus when, according to Luke 2. 22ff, he was taken to the Temple in Jerusalem to be circumcised in accordance with the Law of Moses.

The Christmas season ends on 6th January with the feast of Epiphany, a Greek word meaning 'manifestation'. Originally this marked the baptism of Jesus, as it still does in the East. Today in the West it commemorates the arrival of the Magi or Wise Men at the stable.

There are many symbols, customs and traditions connected with the celebration of Christmas. For hundreds of years before the birth of Jesus people had held celebrations at the winter solstice on December 22nd. The word solstice means 'the sun standing still' and the winter solstice occurs at the shortest day of the year, a time when long ago it was feared the lack of sunshine would cause crops to fail. Boughs of evergreen were hung in homes as a reminder that there was life when many plants and trees seemed to be dead.

Today the celebration of Christmas incorporates some of the symbolism of the midwinter pre-Christian festivities with the festival of Jesus's birth. But over the years the meanings of many of the symbols have changed. The traditional Christmas carol, 'The Holly and the Ivy' is a fine example of this.

The crib

In many churches and homes a nativity scene is displayed which includes the main characters mentioned in the birth narratives, with a baby as the focal point.

Nativity plays

In times past when many people were unable to read, Bible stories were often presented as plays and today many schools and churches continue this tradition with Nativity plays.

Light

Candles are often used in Catholic, Anglican and Orthodox Churches. They are traditionally blessed on Candlemas Day, 2nd February. For Christians, candles are a symbol that Jesus is the Light of the World. Advent candles are used during the four weeks of preparation before the festival of Christmas. Some churches have Advent rings, four candles in a circle of evergreen. One candle is lit each Sunday in Advent. A fifth candle in the centre is lit on Christmas Day.

At home Advent candles may be used. They are marked and one portion is burnt for each day in Advent. One of the traditional celebrations of Advent in Great Britain is a Christingle service in Church. The children of the congregation are given a candle stuck into an orange which is decorated with fruit, sweets and a red ribbon.

Evergreens

Evergreens were used long ago to decorate homes during the winter time as a reminder that life continued during the coldest days of winter. Plants with berries were especially popular since the fruit gave the promise of new life in the spring. Holly has associations with the birth and death of Jesus. The white flower represents the purity of Jesus's mother, Mary; the prickles are a reminder of the crown of thorns placed on Jesus's head at his crucifixion; the red berries are a symbol of the drops of blood and the bitterness of the bark of the tree represents the suffering of Jesus on the cross (see the carol 'The Holly and the Ivy').

Christmas tree

The Christmas tree was introduced to Great Britain by Prince Albert in the middle of the nineteenth century. Prince Albert was a German Prince who became Queen Victoria's husband.

Albert had heard how Martin Luther, a famous Christian, decorated a tree in remembrance of a story told about St Boniface. Boniface was an Englishman who went to Germany in the eighth century to teach about Christianity. One December he found a group of people standing beneath an oak tree preparing to sacrifice a child to a pagan god. Boniface rescued the child, chopped down the tree and replaced it with a small fir tree which he called 'The Tree of the Christ Child'.

Today decorating a tree with a star is a reminder of the star which guided the Magi to the birthplace of Jesus. The tinsel represents an ancient early Christian story about a poor woman who worked very hard to provide for her family. One night a spider spun its web on the family's Christmas tree and as a reward for the woman's goodness, the Christ Child turned the web to silver.

Mistletoe

Mistletoe is used as a symbol of love. The first Christians hung it in their homes and exchanged a kiss underneath it as a reminder of the teaching of Jesus to his disciples about loving one another.

Biblical references

Event	Reference
The announcement of the birth of John the Baptist	Luke 1. 5–25
The Annunciation	Luke 1. 26–38
Mary's visit to Elizabeth	Luke 1. 39–56
The Birth of John the Baptist	Luke 1. 57–80
The Birth of Jesus	Matthew 2. 1–12
The Birth of Jesus and the visit of the Shepherds	Luke 2. 1–20
The visit of the Magi	Matthew 2. 1–12
The Flight into Egypt and the Massacre of the Holy Innocents	Matthew 2. 13–18
The Circumcision of Jesus and the Presentation in the Temple	Luke 2. 21–40

NB All the major events of Christmas are recorded in the Gospels. However, both St John and St Mark begin with the baptism of Jesus and the role of St John the Baptist. The story of the birth of Jesus is to be found only in St Matthew and St Luke.

Christmas

Knowledge of Christian belief and practice

- The Church as a Christian community and a building.

- Types of writing in the Bible: stories; poems; sayings.

- The Bible as two testaments – old and new.

- Key Christian values: courage; forgiveness; self-sacrifice; commitment; love; justice.

- Jesus represented as 'The Light of the World'.

- The celebration of Jesus's birth which shows he is special for Christians.

- Stories about the birth of Jesus, illustrating the idea of God as a parent.

Religious perspectives on human experience

Pupils should be encouraged to explore:

- the importance of belonging to a family group/community;

- special times of the year e.g. birthdays, festivals, St Nicholas, St Lucia;

- families: key figures, birth of a baby;

- why some events are puzzling and why questions may be difficult to answer;

- giving and receiving gifts;

- preparations for key events e.g. journeys.

Learning experiences

Pupils could:

- listen to and respond to stories of Jesus's birth through literature, art, music;

- listen to and be given an opportunity to join in Christmas carols;

- talk about the commercialisation of Christmas;

- visit a variety of Christian places of worship and learn the names of the key features e.g. font, table/altar, pulpit;

- look at and explore symbols of Christmas and Advent: Advent candles/wreath, manger/crib;

- find out how Christian communities celebrate Christmas around the world.

Symbols and artifacts

- Advent candles / Advent wreath / light and darkness
- crib
- nativity plays

EUCHARIST

The most characteristic act of worship in Christian churches is a sacred meal known by various names:

Eucharist
Holy Communion
The Lord's Supper
Mass
Breaking of Bread

Eucharist

The word Eucharist means 'thanksgiving'. Christians follow Jesus's example by giving thanks for the bread and wine which are the fruits of the harvest and the work of humankind. They also give thanks for the gift which Jesus gave of himself at the Last Supper and on the cross.

Holy Communion

The sharing of bread and wine emphasises the fellowship of all those who believe in Jesus.

The Lord's Supper

This emphasises the way in which Christians meet together to obey the command of Jesus to: 'Do this in memory of me'. The word 'supper' is representative of 'fellowship'.

The Breaking of Bread

This title describes the worship of Christians today who follow the example of the first Christians who 'spent their time in learning from the apostles, taking part in the fellowship, and sharing in the fellowship meals and prayers' (Acts 2. 42).

Mass

The word Mass is taken from the Latin word 'missa' which means 'ended' or 'finished'. The Mass is a sacred meal of thanksgiving which shows the unity of the church through Communion with Jesus.

During the act of worship the congregation receives token amounts of bread and wine as a means of 'communion' with one another. Christians believe that by doing this they are following the instructions of Jesus to his disciples at the Last Supper. (Mark 14. 12–26; Luke 22. 7–28; Matthew 26. 17–30). The bread is usually in the form of small unleavened wafers, or small pieces of bread. Some groups of Christians do not use wine but prefer a non-alcoholic juice. At the end of the celebration the priest dismisses the people with the words, 'Go in peace to love and serve the Lord'. Not all Christians use the sacrament however e.g. The Salvation Army and the Society of Friends, and the service varies widely between different Christian groups.

The Orthodox Church

In the Orthodox tradition those who are to receive Holy Communion gather in the centre of the church. The wine is administered by the priest from a chalice into the mouth of each communicant and he says the name of each person to whom he administers the sacrament. It is usual to fast for a period of time up to one day before receiving Communion.

The Baptist Church

In the Baptist tradition the bread and wine is blessed by the minister and administered by deacons to the congregation who pass the plate of bread from one to another, each person taking a piece and consuming it immediately. Non-alcoholic wine is administered in individual glasses and consumed as a corporate act to symbolise that Christians are the body of Christ who share in communion together.

The Roman Catholic Church

In the Roman Catholic Church Christians believe that the sacrifice of Jesus for the forgiveness of sins is represented in the sacrament. The chalice is not however given at all services.

The Anglican Church

At the Communion service in the Anglican Church (Church of England) the people come before the altar or Communion table and receive first bread and then wine from a single chalice (or cup).

Eucharist

Knowledge of Christian belief and practice

- The Church as a Christian community.
- Keeping Sunday as a holy day.
- The importance of special times to the Christian community.
- Worshipping together: reading the Bible; praying.
- Special leaders e.g. priests; ministers; elders.

- Christian values: Jesus's teaching on forgiveness and love; relationships with family and friends.

- Different names for the sacred meal: Eucharist; Holy Communion; Lord's Supper; Holy Liturgy; Mass; Breaking Bread.

Religious perspectives on human experience

Pupils should be encouraged to explore:

- what it is like to belong to a group;

- how we remember people when we are separated from them;

- people who set an example;

- how we say 'sorry';

- meals and celebrations which are special to them;

- books and other objects at home which are special or have special significance.

Learning experiences

Pupils could:

- look and handle artifacts which are used in Christian worship;

- bake bread and share it with friends;

- share feelings about values which might be important to them e.g. forgiveness, kindness, loyalty;

- talk about important figures in their own lives;

- write a 'thank you' prayer, a 'sorry' prayer, prayers for ourselves and other people;

- visit a church and learn the names of the key features e.g. altar/table, pulpit, font, lectern;

- listen to music from a sung Eucharist.

Symbols and artifacts

- bread
- wine
- cross/crucifix
- chalice/cup
- altar/table
- candles
- Bible
- prayer book /order of service/missal
- liturgical colours
- water

PENTECOST OR WHITSUN

The narrative in Acts recounts how forty days after his resurrection Jesus was taken back to heaven in bodily form.

> When the apostles sat together with Jesus, they asked him, 'Lord at this time will you give the kingdom back to Israel?' Jesus said to them, 'The times and occasions are set by my father's own authority, and it is not for you to know when they will be. But when the Holy Spirit comes upon you, you will be filled with power, and you will be witnesses for me in Jerusalem, in all Judea and Samaria and to the ends of the earth.' After saying this, he was taken up to heaven as they watched him, and a cloud hid him from their sight. They still had their eyes fixed on the sky as he went away, when two men dressed in white suddenly stood beside them and said, 'Galileans, why are you standing there looking up into the sky? This Jesus, who was taken from you to heaven, will come back in the same way that you saw him go to heaven.
>
> Acts 1. 6–11

Ten days later in Acts we read:

> When the day of Pentecost came, all the believers were gathered together in one place. Suddenly there was a noise from the sky which sounded like a strong wind blowing, and it filled the whole house where they were sitting. Then they saw what looked like tongues of fire which spread out and touched each person. They were all filled with the Holy Spirit and began to talk in other languages, as the Spirit enabled them to speak.

> There were Jews living in Jerusalem, religious men who had come from every country in the world. When they heard this noise a large crowd gathered. They were all excited, because each of them heard the believers speaking in his own language. In amazement and wonder they exclaimed: 'These people are talking like they are Galileans! How is it, then, that all of us hear them speaking in our own native language? We are from all over the world yet all of us hear them speaking in our own languages about the great things that God has done!' Amazed and confused they asked each other, 'What does this mean?'

> Acts 2. 1–12

It is this event which is remembered on Pentecost Day when the first Christians began to carry out the mission which Jesus left them. The festival is often referred to as 'the birthday of the Church'.

There are two concepts which are crucial to understanding Pentecost and the associated events. These are *Trinity* and *The Holy Spirit.*

Trinity

Christians believe there is one God and that God exists in three persons, Father, Son and Holy Spirit, though being one in substance. This belief is often referred to as a mystery. In other words, it cannot be explained or fully understood by human reason.

49

The Trinity is made explicit in St Matthew's Gospel when the apostles were instructed to baptise in the name of the Father, Son and Spirit (Matthew 28. 19). In St Luke's accounts of the annunciation and of Jesus's baptism, belief in the Trinity is inferred by reference to the Holy Spirit (Luke 1. 35).

Holy Spirit

The third person of the Trinity is the Holy Spirit. Some Christians describe the Holy Spirit as the 'Power of God'. There are many references in the Old Testament to the Holy Spirit. These have their beginnings in the account of the creation when 'the Spirit of God moved over the waters' (Genesis 1. 2). Christians also find reference to the Holy Spirit in the Servant Songs of Isaiah (Isaiah 40 ff). In the New Testament, St Luke writes of the power of the Spirit at the Annunciation (Luke 1. 35); at Jesus's baptism (Mark 1. 10) and during the temptations of Jesus (Mark 1. 12).

Often Christians speak of the fruits or gifts of the Holy Spirit.

Fruits of the Spirit	*Gifts of the Spirit*
Love	Wisdom
Joy	Understanding
Peace	Counsel
Patience	Courage
Kindness	Knowledge
Goodness	Piety
Faithfulness	Reverence of the Lord
Gentleness	
Self-control	

Pentecost – Whitsun

Knowledge of Christian belief and practice

- Key Christian values: love, joy, peace, patience, kindness, goodness, faithfulness, gentleness, self-control, wisdom, understanding, counsel, courage, knowledge, piety, reverence of the Lord.

- The Church as a Christian community and a building.

- Events from Jesus's life as told in the Gospel narratives and the Acts of the Apostles.

- The celebration of key events in Jesus's life throughout the year.

- Language/symbols which describe God as The Holy Trinity.

- Commitment, shared identity and belief of the Holy Spirit seen through baptism and the Eucharist.

- Considering attitudes to personal issues which relate to the gifts and fruits of the spirit.

Religious perspectives on human experience

Pupils should be encouraged to explore:

- the importance of belonging to a family group/community;

- special times of the year e.g. festivals;

- families: key figures; birth/birthdays;

- why some concepts are puzzling and why questions may be difficult to answer;

- giving and accepting gifts;

- the experience of fire, water, power, wind in everyday life;

- caring for humankind and the world around;

- personal qualities e.g. patience, kindness, goodness, self-control, courage.

Learning experiences

Pupils could:

- listen to and respond to stories of Jesus's Ascension and Pentecost;

- discuss their experience of belonging to a community e.g. home, school, worshipping community;

- explore positive and destructive forces of wind and fire in the world;

- explore the dove as a symbol of peace;

- visit a Christian place of worship which is decorated for Pentecost;

- discover how different Christian communities celebrate the birthday of the Church e.g. Whit walks, shared meal;

- think about how they might share the gifts and fruits of the spirit with other people.

Symbols and artifacts

- dove
- fire
- water
- wind
- colour – gold, red, white
- Trinitarian symbols

SUKKOT

Sukkot or Tabernacles is celebrated by Jews from the fifteenth to the twenty second day of the Hebrew month of Tishri. The festival commemorates the time when the Israelites lived in tents or booths during their wanderings for nearly forty years in the wilderness before reaching the Promised Land where they became an independent nation.

Long ago the festival was one when people made a pilgrimage to Jerusalem. When the pilgrims caught their first sight of the temple they shouted for joy and sang psalms. The high priest would fill a pitcher with water from the pool of Siloam and this was later poured onto the temple altar whilst people processed waving willow branches. During the evenings four tall menorah (candlesticks) were lit in the court of the women as a focal point for singing and dancing. On the last day of the celebrations when the water was poured onto the stone altar, the congregation processed seven times around it beating the willow branches on the ground and offering prayers for rain to bring a good harvest.

Today Jewish families erect a sukkah or hut for the festival. Meals are usually eaten there but it is also used for sleeping in if the weather is fine. The temporary structure of the sukkah is a reminder that the children of Israel were only able to live in safety in the booths because of the protection of God. Many synagogues have a communal sukkah for people who are unable to construct their own.

There are specific rules concerning the structure of a sukkah. Firstly, it should be a temporary building, ideally constructed each year. However, if the frame or walls are left up from one year to the next, then the roof should be made new and it should be the last part of the building to be completed. The ceiling should be made of plant material 'grown from the earth' which is 'cut down' for this purpose and the sky should remain visible though parts of it. The sukkah should be sufficiently large to live in, and of a specified height. A sukkah is decorated inside with fruits such as oranges, apples and grapes, bottles of oil and water and little boxes containing sweet meats. This fulfils God's command that 'the festival should be celebrated with joy'. Pictures of Israel past and present may be hung on the walls.

Each evening during the festival, the table is set for a meal which will include Challah bread (plaited loaves). Candles are lit by the woman of the house as she recites a special blessing on the family.

It is customary to set an extra place at table for one of the great Biblical characters of the past (e.g. Abraham, Isaac, Joseph, Moses, David, Aaron) as a reminder of the part they played in the Jewish religion.

Sukkot is also known as 'The Festival of Ingathering' in the Bible, for, once settled in Canaan the Hebrews not only remembered the time when they wandered in the wilderness but also gave thanks to God for the gathering in of crops in their new land.

There are four symbols which are closely connected with Sukkot. These are branches of palm, myrtle and willow, together with a citrus fruit like a lemon (etrog). The symbols are still used during Sukkot services. A palm branch decorated with willow and myrtle is held in the right hand and a citron in the left.

There are several explanations concerning the four symbols. Firstly the citron is said to represent the heart; the palm the spine; the myrtle the eye and the willow the lips. The four symbols joined together represent people living together in harmony in God's presence. Secondly, that taste represents learning; smell represents good deeds: the etrog has taste and smell; the myrtle has smell but no taste; the willow and palm have neither taste nor smell. Each therefore represents a different kind of person. Some have learning and do good deeds; some have one or the other; and some have neither. Fellowship with God requires all personalities to be together.

SIMHAT TORAH

The last day of Sukkot is called Simhat Torah or 'The Rejoicing of the Torah'. The festival marks the end of the yearly cycle of the readings from the Torah and it bears witness that for hundreds of years Jews have read the Hebrew scriptures. In the synagogue the last portion of Deuteronomy is read and the first part of Genesis. The scrolls are removed from the Ark and processed around the synagogue.

In addition to the Torah being honoured, the synagogue congregation also honours two of its members. They are invited to be 'bridegrooms' for the day. In Orthodox synagogues this is restricted to men, but Progressive synagogues honour both men and women. The person selected to read the final part of Deuteronomy is called 'Chatan Torah' (bridegroom of the Torah), and the person who reads the first part of Genesis is named 'Chatan Beraysheet' (bridegroom of Genesis). When women are honoured they are usually called Kala (bride).

Simhat Torah is of special significance to children who learn from its ceremonies the importance of the Torah in the lives of Jewish people throughout the world. It is a time to join in processions around the synagogue carrying banners, flags and candles while traditional songs and psalms are sung.

Sukkot

Knowledge of Jewish belief and practice

- Israel as a special place for Jews; a uniting factor in Jewish life.
- Family and community life.
- Special places: home, synagogue, sukkah.
- Special times: shabbat and the shabbat night meal; pilgrim festivals.
- Stories in the Torah which describe God as Creator and sustainer.
- Rules and codes of behaviour.
- Responsibility to God – the Shema, mezuzah, tallit, kippah, the Ten Commandments.
- Jewish identity expressed through worship and celebration.

Religious perspectives on human experience

Pupils should be encouraged to explore:

- homes they know;

- what is important in their own lives;
- special occasions and places in their own lives;
- shared family meals;
- the importance of doing things together;
- the dependence / interdependence of the world / humankind.

Learning experiences

Pupils could:

- share feelings about the importance of families and friends, gratitude, thanksgiving;
- talk about special times and occasions in their own lives;
- listen to passages from the Torah or songs and psalms associated with Sukkot;
- discover how people express their identity;
- watch a video of a Jewish family celebrating Sukkot;
- design a miniature Sukkot and decorate it;
- hear some of the prayers used during Sukkot and talk about the feelings and beliefs they express.

Symbols and artifacts

- tallit
- kippar
- sukkah
- etrog, myrtle, willow, palm, lulav

DIVALI

Divali is an important Hindu festival of light which takes place during October or November in the Western calendar. Most Hindus celebrate the festival but in some regions it is of particular importance to businessmen and to bankers, since one of the main events is the worship of Lakshmi, goddess of wealth in Hindu mythology.

The word Divali is an abbreviation for the word Deepavali, meaning a row of lights and it celebrates the coronation of Rama and Sita.

Common elements of the festival will include cleaning and decorating the family home; sharing meals with family and friends, the giving and receiving of gifts, illuminating homes and pathways with rows of lights (divas) and worship.

Each day of the festival is set aside for different aspects of worship and celebration.

Day 1: the 13th day of the month of Ashwin

A single diva lamp is lit and placed in a south facing position at the front of the house, as an offering to Yama, God of death. At other times of the year lamps face north or east.

Day 2: the 14th day of the month of Ashwin

This day celebrates the victory of Krishna over the demon Narakaasura. Many people will rise early and bath, using perfumed oils. New clothes are worn and often breakfast is shared with relatives and friends. Often spicy or sweet foods are eaten, firecrackers are let off and oil lamps are lit at night.

Day 3: the 15th day of the month of Ashwin

On this day the goddess Lakshmi is worshipped and doors and windows may be left open to allow her in. Patterns from rice and flour may be made on floors and numerous oil lamps are lit in order that Lakshmi will be able to see her way should she visit the house.

Bankers and businessmen finalise their accounts for the end of the financial year and many ordinary folk will make sure their bills are paid.

Day 4: the first day of the month of Kartik

On this day married women often receive a gift of jewellery from their husband. There is feasting and presents may be exchanged between family and friends. The new financial year begins.

Day 5: the second day of the month of Kartik

This is known as Sisters' Day. Men are forbidden to eat food cooked by their wives and are encouraged to visit their sisters who welcome them with sweetmeats. A ceremonial bath may take place with sisters rubbing scented oils onto the head, back and arms of their brothers. A dot of red powder (kumkum) is often placed on the forehead of a brother by his sister and a lamp moved in a circular motion before him to warn off evil spirits. Afterwards sisters are often given a gift before returning home.

Knowledge of Hindu belief and practice

- Devotion to God.
- God represented in different forms through images e.g. Rama, Sita, Lakshmi.
- The community as a family.
- Festival foods.
- Stories of Rama and Sita (Ramayana) and on the theme of good and evil.
- Names of some of the scriptures and how they are used by adherents.

Religious perspectives on human experience

Pupils should be encouraged to think about:

- family customs and traditions;
- giving and receiving gifts;
- different communities to which they belong;
- special times and shared occasions;
- when they have special food;
- favourite stories and characters;
- what they mean by good and evil.

Learning experiences

Pupils could:

- share feelings about family and friends;
- find out about life in India;
- talk about how people have different personalities and how the same person may have different values;
- watch a video of a Divali celebration;
- listen to and respond to stories from the Ramayana;
- make rangoli patterns and designs, masks for characters in Rama and Sita story, thumb pots from clay for divas;
- think about new beginnings in their own lives.

Symbols and artifacts

- symbol of Aum
- images of Rama, Sita, Hanuman, Lakshmi
- fire
- light and darkness

PUJA

'Puja' is the Hindu word for showing honour and reverence to God. Many Hindu homes will have a separate place or shrine where puja is performed. The items used to perform the ceremony will be kept there together with images of one or more of the deities and other sacred symbols such as the Hindu syllable, Aum.

In preparation for puja a Hindu will bathe. A bell is rung just before the ceremony begins and incense may be burned to make the air smell sweet. Prayers are then said. These will always include the Gayatri Mantra. Offering of food such as rice, nuts, and sweets are made to the deities and sometimes the images are bathed and a special paste made from sandalwood (kumkum) is applied.

Sometimes worshippers may also make a mark with kumkum on their forehead. This is known as a talak mark.

It is usual for a small lamp to be lit and moved in front of the deity during worship. This part of puja is known as the arti ceremony. Puja is completed when the worshipper bids the deity farewell.

The puja ceremony is full of sensory experiences and therefore the activity is a particularly valuable one.

Knowledge of Hindu belief and practice

- Devotion to God.

- The community as a family.

- Foods associated with Hindu worship and celebration.

- God represented in different forms through images.

- Names of some of the scriptures and how they are used by adherents.

- Worship at the home and the Mandir including the importance of cleansing/washing as a preparation.

Religious perspectives on human experience

Pupils should be encouraged to explore:

- family customs and traditions;
- giving and receiving gifts;
- the importance of ritual in everyday life;
- groups to which they belong.

Learning experiences

Pupils could:

- watch a puja ceremony;
- share feelings about the importance of family and friends;
- give and receive gifts;
- find out about life in India;
- explore images of Hindu deities and learn their names;
- reflect upon and experience colours, smells, tastes, rituals associated with the puja ceremony;
- visit a Mandir or a Hindu Shrine;
- find out where their families came from and where they have relatives;
- talk about how people have different personalities and how the same person may have different values.

Symbols and artifacts

- light – divas, sacred fire – arti, havan kund
- foods – offerings, milk, rice, dried fruits, sweetmeats, deities, prashad

RELIGIOUS ARTIFACTS

For thousands of years, humankind has used religious objects and symbols. Artifacts may be central to worship, or used to help direct attention. Sometimes they provide comfort or inspiration, for example, a holy picture, scarred by years of being folded in a pocket, or a Seder plate which has been present in a Jewish family at the reenactment of the Exodus story for generations. Their value is in the symbolic meaning they have for their owners and in the doors which they open to believers and to those who learn from them.

In school, artifacts help children to explore questions and beliefs, giving them the opportunity to learn from direct experience. They may also help to foster communication skills, and they lend themselves as inspiration for the creative and expressive arts in poems, stories and songs.

It is important that all children see and touch religious artifacts, sensing their visual and tactile qualities, for their presence brings a dimension to religion which it is difficult to create through even the best posters, videos and books. But their value does not end here, because they are objects of reflection, used as a focal point in rituals and celebrations, or as aids to prayer and meditation.

But how far should religious objects be used in the context of RE? Perhaps the golden rule is that their use should be to encourage reflection rather than devotion. As teachers, we must tread with great care. The attitudes which we convey to pupils by the way in which we talk about and use artifacts speak a thousand words to children.

Purchasing can be an exciting and rewarding experience. Many local faith communities will have shops where artifacts can be bought. The following suppliers are also recommended.

Artifacts to Order

(Telephone: 01945 587452)

Collections of religious artifacts, arranged in sets.

Articles of Faith

Resource House

Kay Street

Bury BL9 6BU

(Telephone: 0161 763 6232)

Colour brochure of artifacts relating to each principal religion. Also some collections of artifacts based on a theme e.g. Festivals of Light, Passover.

History in Evidence

Unit 7

Monk Road

Alfreton

Derbyshire DE55 7RL

(Telephone: 01773 830255)

Colour brochure with pictures of artifacts relating to principal religions. Artifacts may be ordered separately or in collections.

SPCK Bookshop

7 St Peter's Street

Canterbury CT1 3AT

(Telephone: 01227 462881)

Suppliers of Christian artifacts. NB Check local telephone directory for nearest SPCK shop.

Tantra Designs

Gas Ferry Road

Bristol BS1 6UN

Buddhist images, incense, posters, cards etc.

Little India

91 The Broadway

Southall

Middx UB1 1LN

(Telephone: 0181 571 2029)

Highly recommended for mail order or direct purchase of Hindu, Sikh and Muslim artifacts.

Muslim Information Services

223 Seven Sisters Road

London N4 2DA

(Telephone: 0171 272 5170)

Mail order and direct purchase of Muslim artifacts.

Jewish Memorial Council Bookshop

Woburn House

Upper Woburn Place

Tavistock Square

London WC1H OEP

(Telephone: 0171 387 3952 x 140)

Mail order of Jewish artifacts offering 10 per cent discount for school orders.

Christian artifacts might include:

- chalice (for wine at the Eucharist)
- paten for bread or wafers (at the Eucharist)
- wafers (unconsecrated)
- individual wine glass used in Communion services in Free Churches
- basket used for the bread in Free Church Communion services
- white tablecloth used to cover the Communion table
- icon
- Bibles: family; Gideon New Testament; children's
- Order of Service books: Anglican Book of Common Prayer; Wedding Service; Funeral Service; Baptism Service; Ordination Service; Confirmation Service
- prayer books: Anglican; Roman Catholic Missal; Orthodox; Free Churches
- prayer cards
- hassock
- hymn books; carol sheets
- crosses: wooden; pendant; crucifix; Celtic; palm
- baptism gown
- ichthus badge (fish)
- dove badge
- statue of the Madonna and Child
- badges of Christian organisations
- clerical collar worn by ordained priests and ministers
- rosary

- cards: Easter; Christmas; First Communion; Confirmation; Ordination; Wedding; Sympathy

- confirmation veil

- incense (Prinknash)

- candles: baptism; votive; memorial; vigil; First Communion; Advent

- Advent calendar

- thurible (incense burner)

Jewish artifacts might include:

- kiddush cup (wine goblet for Shabbat)

- Shabbat candlesticks and candles (and a travelling pair if possible)

- Order of service for Shabbat

- challah loaf (plaited loaf used at Shabbat)

- challah bread cover

- spice box for Shabbat

- tallit (prayer shawl)

- siddur (daily prayer book)

- tzizit (fringed undervest worn by some Jewish males)

- tefillin (small leather boxes containing passages from the Torah)

- kippah (yamulkah or capel) – male head covering

- mezuzah and scroll

- Tenach (Jewish Bible)

- Sefer Torah scroll (five books of Moses written on parchment)

- yad (for pointing when reading from scrolls)

- dreidel

- magen David (Star of David)

- Seder dish (Passover dish)

- Hagadah (Pesach service book)

- Pesach cards (Passover cards)

- passover napkins

- Matzot (in the red box marked 'for Passover use')

- Matzah cover

- Jewish New Year card

- Bar-Mitzvah card (male initiation)

- Bat-Mitzvah card (female initiation)

- ketubah (marriage certificate)

- menorah (branched candlestick)

- candles for menorah

- gregger (noise-maker used in Purim celebrations)

- shofar (ram's horn for Rosh Hashanah)

- memorial light

Hindu artifacts might include:

- Aum (Om) symbol representing God

- spices (saffron, cumin and crushed chillies) and container

- henna

- joss sticks (incense sticks)

- packet of cotton wicks (for arti or diva lamps)

- arti lamp; divas

- janeu (sacred thread worn by Hindus who study under a guru)

- rakhi (bracelet made out of silk or cotton)
- puja set and tray
- tarbhana (large copper dish used for worship)
- beaker for holy water
- aachman (spoon)
- copper dish (saucer-shaped) for money offerings
- mala (circle of stringed prayer beads)
- Kirtan or Bhajans (copies of devotional hymns)
- har (garland used for decoration, adornment, ceremonies and festivals)
- kumkum (red powder)
- bindi (red spots for forehead)
- dhoti (garment made of natural fibre worn by males)
- pictures of Hindu deities
- figures of Hindu deities (Ganesha, Hanuman, Krishna, Lakshmi, Parvati, Shiva, Vishnu, Rama, Sita)
- book of rangoli patterns

APPENDIX 1

Possible Aims for the RE Programme in the Primary School

Religious Education will, through a programme in which pupils *learn about* religion and *learn from* religion, provide opportunities for each pupil to:

1. explore some religious beliefs and some of the practices associated with them;

2. recognise the importance of religious belief and practice;

3. begin to develop an understanding and awareness of concepts in religion;

4. foster an enquiring approach to aspects of religion;

5. develop and discuss their own beliefs and values;

6. raise perceptive questions and therefore:

7. understand religion.

Ten Silver Rules for RE in the School

1. If we are going to tell a story from a religious tradition, we should have read it beforehand.

2. We should ensure we have sufficient control of the information we are going to use.

3. We should have clear aims and objectives for the activity.

4. We will remember that religions differ between and within themselves.

5. We will treat all views with respect but not necessarily avoid contentious issues and sometimes take risks.

6. We will set our own opinions to one side while the pupils begin to develop their own insight and understanding at their own level.

7. We will remember that not everyone believes all religions end up in the same place.

8. We will be prepared to confess ignorance if necessary!

9. We will remember that our own views should not inhibit pupils' learning.

10. We will remember that teaching and learning in RE can be not only interesting but enjoyable too!

Further Reading and Resources

The following books provide information about the principal religions. Schools should choose from each section and keep a record of selected titles in the documentation which provides information about resources for Religious Education.

CHRISTIANITY

F. Brossier and Manneron, *A First Bible: Old Testament*, Simon & Schuster, 1988.

F. Brossier and Manneron, *New Testament*, Simon & Schuster, 1989.

W. O. Cole and R. Mantin, *Teaching Christianity*, Heinemann, 1994.

T. Cooling, *Concept Cracking – Exploring Christian Beliefs in School*, Stapleford Project, 1994.

T. de Paola, *Tomie de Paola's Book of Bible Stories*, Hodder & Stoughton, 1990.

J. Drane, *Christians – Through the Ages – Around the World*, Lion Publishing, 1994.

C. Fewins, *Be a Church Detective*, Church House Publishing, 1992.

R. O. Hughes, *Christianity: Religions Through Festivals*, Longman, 1989.

M. Killingray and J. Killingray, *I am an Anglican*, Franklin Watts, 1986.

B. Pettenuzzo, *I am a Roman Catholic*, Franklin Watts, 1985.

B. Pettenuzzo, *I am a Pentecostal*, Franklin Watts, 1986.

M. Roussou, *I am a Greek Orthodox*, Franklin Watts, 1985.

JUDAISM

M. Austerberry, *The Westhill Project RE 5–6 – JEWS 1 and 2*, Stanley Thornes, 1990.

A. Clark and S. Malyan (ed.), *Passover Seder for Primary Schools*, Wandsworth Borough Council, 1990.

L. Harrigan, *Celebrations: Sam's Passover*, A & C Black, 1985.

J. Koralek, *Hanukkah – The Festival of Lights*, Walker Books, 1989.

C. Lawton and C. Fairclough, *I am a Jew*, Franklin Watts, 1984.

J. Patherson, *A Happy New Year*, Hamish Hamilton, 1987.

J. Patherson, *Mazal-Tov: A Jewish Wedding*, Hamish Hamilton, 1988.

S. R. Topek, *Ten Good Rules*, Kar-Ben Copies Inc, 1991.

J. Wood, *Our Culture*, Franklin Watts, 1988.

ISLAM

M. Aggarwal and C. Fairclough, *I am a Muslim*, Franklin Watts, 1985.

J. Ardavan, *Growing up in Islam*, Longman, 1990.

M. Davies, *The Life of Muhammad*, Wayland, 1987.

D. Hart, *Leaders of Religion – Muhammad*, Oliver & Boyd, 1985.

R. Kerven, *Festival! Ramdan and Eid-ul-Fitr*, Macmillan Education, 1986.

H. Khattab, *Stories from the Muslim World*, Macdonald, 1987.

J. Mayled, *Muslim Festivals*, RMEP, 1990.

The Prophets, IQRA Trust, 1992.

HINDUISM

M. Aggarwal and G. Goswami, *I am a Hindu*, Franklin Watts, 1984.

P. Bahree, *The Hindu World*, Macdonald, 1989.

O. Bennett, *Festival! Diwali*, Macmillan Education, 1986.

O. Bennett, *Holi: Hindu Festival of Spring*, Hamish Hamilton, 1987.

J. Gavin, *Stories from the Hindu World*, Macdonald, 1986.

J. S. Hirst, *The Story of the Hindus*, OUP, 1989.

J. Hirst and G. Pandey, *Growing up in Hinduism*, Longman, 1990.

R. Jackson, *Religions through Festivals – Hinduism*, Longman, 1988.

V. P. Kanitkar, *Indian Food and Drink*, Wayland, 1986.

V. P. Kanitkar, *Religious Stories – Hindu Stories*, Wayland, 1986.

P. Mitchell, *Dance of Shiva*, Hamish Hamilton, 1989.

S. Mitter, *Festivals – Hindu Festivals*, Wayland, 1985.

L. Shanson and A. Chowdry, *Journey with the Gods*, Matra, 1987.

SIKHISM

M. Aggarwal, *I am a Sikh*, Franklin Watts, 1984.

R. Arora, *Guru Nanak and the Sikh Gurus*, Wayland, 1987.

A. Clutterbuck, *Growing up in Sikhism*, Longman, 1990.

S. Lyle, *Pavan is a Sikh*, A & C Black, 1977.

R. Singh and J. Singh, *Stories from the Sikh World*, Macdonald, 1987.

Teaching RE – Sikhism 5–11, CEM, 1994.

BUDDHISM

A. Bancroft, *Festivals of the Buddha*, RMEP, 1984.

R. Brown and P. Emmett, *The Budda and the Elephant*, Mary Glasgow Publications, 1989.

J. Landaw and J. Brooke, *Prince Siddhartha*, Wisdom, 1980.

D. Samarasekara, *I am a Buddhist*, Franklin Watts, 1986.

J. Snelling, *Buddhist Festivals*, Wayland, 1985.

J. Snelling, *Buddhism*, Wayland, 1986.

J. Snelling, *Buddhist Stories*, Wayland, 1986.

J. Snelling, *The Life of the Budda*, Wayland, 1987.

J. Wood, *Our Culture – Buddist*, Franklin Watts, 1988.

GENERAL

D. Bastide, *Good Practice in Primary Religious Education 4–11*, The Falmer Press, 1992.

E. Broeilly and M. Palmer, *Religions of the World*, Sainsbury Harper Collins, 1993.

A. Brown and E. Brown, *Primary School Worship*, National Society, 1992.

M. Cooling, *Faith History – Ideas for RE, History and Assembly in the Primary School*, Eagle Publishing, 1994.

C. Erricker (ed.), *Teaching World Religions*, The Shap Working Party, 1993.

Folens Primary RE Programme and Topic Pack, catalogue available from Folens Publishers, Albert House, Apex Business Centre, Boscombe Road, Dunstable, LU5 4RL

M. Grimmitt, J. Grove and L. Spencer, *A Gift To The Child*, Simon & Schuster, 1991.

C. Howard, *Investigating Artefacts*, RMEP, 1995.

Nelson Living Religions, RE course for Primary schools, catalogue available from Thomas Nelson Customer Services, Freepost, ITPS Ltd, North Way, Andover, Hants, SP10 5BR.

J. Palmer, *Blueprints – Festivals*, Stanley Thornes, 1993.

R. Parmiter, *Blueprints – Religious Education Key Stage 1*, Stanley Thornes, 1993.

R. Parmiter, *Blueprints – Religious Education Key Stage 1 – Teacher's Resource Book*, Stanley Thornes, 1993.

J. Rankin, A. Brown and M. Hayward, *Religious Education Topics for the Primary School*, Longman, 1989.

J. Rankin, A. Brown and M. Hayward, *Religious Education Across the Curriculum*, Longman, 1991.

G. Read, J. Rudge, G. Teece and R. Howarth, *The Westhill Project RE 5–16 – How do I Teach RE?*, Stanley Thornes, 1986.

M. Stone, *Don't Just Do Something Sit There*, RMEP, 1995.

G. Teece, *Religious Artefacts in the Classroom*, Hodder & Stoughton, 1992.

G. Teece, *How to Write your School Policy for RE*, Westhill RE Centre, 1994.

The Warwick RE Project, *Bridges to Religions*, Heinemann, 1995.

MULTIMEDIA

Eggshells and Thunderbolts, multimedia resources for primary RE, with focus on Christianity (video, audio cassettes and CD), BBC Education and Culham College Institute, available from BBC Educational Development, PO Box 50, Wetherby, West Yorkshire LS23 7EZ.

Living Stones, a multimedia CD-Rom and manual on the history of Christianity in Britain. Available from Ms Carol Robinson, Culham College Institute, 60 East St Helen Street, Abingdon, Oxon OX14 5EB, telephone 01235 520458.

POSTERS, WALLCHARTS AND ARTIFACTS

see also the addresses listed on p. 63.

The Buddhist Society
58 Eccleston Square
London SW1V 1PH
Tel: 0171 834 5858
Wide selection of audio tapes for
purchase. Catalogue available.

Christian Education Movement
Royal Buildings
Victoria Street
Derby DE3 1GW
Tel: 01332 296655
A comprehensive collection of booklets
and posters. Brochure available.

Degh Tegh Fateh
117 Soho Road
Handsworth
Birmingham B21 9ST
Tel: 0121 515 1183
All kinds of Sikh religious artifacts,
books and audio visual resources

Folens Publishers
Albert House, Apex Business Centre
Boscombe Road
Dunstable LU5 4RL
Tel: 01582 472788
Photopacks and posterpacks.
Brochure available.

Gohil Emporium
381 Stratford Road
Sparkhill
Birmingham B11 4JZ
Tel: 0121 771 3048
Religious artifacts from India - price
lists available

ISKON Educational Services
Bhativedanta Manor
Letchmore Heath
Watford
Herts WD2A 8EP
Tel: 01923 857244
Hindu artifacts and other resources

The Islamic Cultural Centre and
London Central Mosque
146 Park Road
London NW8 7RG
Tel: 0171 724 3363

The Jewish Education Bureau
8 Westcombe Avenue
Leeds LS8 2BS
Tel: 0113 293 3523
Brochure of resources and services available

Minaret House
9 Leslie Park Road
Croydon
Surrey CR0 6TN
Tel: 0181 681 2972
Islamic visual aid material.

The Respect Journal
7 Elyham
Purley-on-Thames
Reading
Berks RG8 8EN
Tel: 01734 843664

Philip Green Educational Limited
PGE, 112a Alcester Road
Studley
Warwickshire BV80 7NR
Tel: 01527 854711
Picture packs, slide-sets and filmstrips

St Paul Multimedia Centre
199 Kensington High Street
London W8 6BA
Tel: 0171 937 9591
*Roman Catholic Centre with a
wide range of Christian materials
for religious education. Branches
also in Birmingham, Liverpool
and Glasgow.*

Pictorial Charts Educational Trust
PCET, 27 Kirchen Road
London W13 0UD
Tel: 0181 567 9206
*A wide variety of pictures, posters and
wallcharts. Brochure available.*

The Westhill Project
Westhill RE Centre
Westhill College, Selly Oak
Birmingham B29 6LL
Tel: 0121 472 7248
Poster packs on all the major world faiths.

Religion in Evidence
Unit 7
Monk Road
Alfreton
Derbyshire DE55 7RL
Tel: 01773 830255
Religious artifacts and posters.